How To Prepare for and Make the Most of a TV News Appearance

Introduction

Whether you're a student in the field, just starting out as a public relations pro, or a practitioner with lots of experience who needs some refreshers, I intend to provide you with practical advice and down-to-earth tips.

Contents

1.

Feed the Advance Info

Congrats, PR pro! Your carefully crafted pitch has hit home, and you've secured your client a segment on the local television station's news program. Now what? Securing the segment is not where your job ends. Quite the contrary. A segment on the local news is a golden opportunity to get the word out about your client's product, service, or event, and the worst thing you can do is squander it. Mishandling this appearance could do damage to your client's brand, as well as to your own reputation.

Remember, every interaction you have with a member of the media reflects on you and adds to your reputation as a media relations rep. You want to become known as the one who offers interesting news items and segments, shows up on time and well-prepared, is easy to work with and reliable, and doesn't take media coverage for granted. Depending on the circumstances, your client may not interact with these particular producers, reporters, camera operators, or news anchors ever again, but you almost certainly will.

You should be able to tell fairly early on how each individual you're in contact with at the station prefers to be reached—by phone (unlikely), email (probably), or text (increasingly). If you're not sure, don't be afraid to ask, "Is this the best way to reach you?" Stick to the method that seems to get the quickest response back from them.

As soon as your segment is confirmed, send the producer or planner who booked you as much relevant information about the segment as you can. Clearly identify each person who will be interviewed, and their official titles. It's okay to have more than one speaking guest, if absolutely necessary, but try to keep it to two at the most, unless it's a long, multi-part segment, and you and the producer have agreed ahead of time to feature several guests.

Next, include a short list of talking points that are the most important for your client to get across, and would be most interesting to the TV audience. Some producers or reporters/anchors will have their own points to make, but more often than not, they want some guidance from you. Live TV is all about using time wisely, so it's important that they know the key points you want to get across in the couple of minutes you've been allotted. (Make sure your client also knows what those bullet points are, and you have both agreed on them beforehand.)

If there are any words or names that might come up in your segment that are difficult to pronounce, include a pronunciation guide.

Finally, indicate clearly the information that should appear on the screen to accompany your segment. That would usually be the name, date, and time of your event, the name of the organization/business, and the website URL to visit for more information. (Often, the TV station will put its own website up instead, with a link to your website, to increase its own web traffic.) If there's room and it's important, include a phone number the public can call for information or to make a purchase/donation.

Working at the Opera, we had all kinds of foreign words and names we had to help the interviewers pronounce. One time, a young reporter got the idea that the conductor's first name was "Maestro." I waited a beat too long to correct her, and by then it was too late. Luckily, the maestro took it with good humor.

2.
Deliver the Supporting Materials

Think about what the TV producer needs to make the segment work. Examples of items you might need to get into their hands ahead of time are electronic press kits, b-roll (supporting video footage), digital images, or music files. Email these to the station early and identify them very clearly with the scheduled segment date and the producer's name. Follow up to make sure the producer received them and see whether they need anything else.

If a file is too large to email, use Dropbox or a similar sharing platform, and send a link to the producer to download it. You can either keep the folder private or protect it with a password that you give to the producer. You can change the password each time you do this, if necessary.

TV stations can be chaotic places. You can imagine the number of submissions they receive, both solicited and un-, and the number of memory sticks, DVDs, press kits, and packages delivered on any given day. Things get lost all the time. It's not their responsibility to keep track of your stuff. Don't send them anything you would miss if you didn't get it back (such as the *only* copy of your client's background music, for example).

3.
Reconfirm the Segment

Check in with the producer to reconfirm the details of your segment the day before it's scheduled. It's better to do this by email, so you have a written record of the confirmation. Be sure to frame your email to make it obvious that you expect a response. Here are a couple of examples of sign-offs:

```
Please confirm that we have the correct time! Looking forward to
it.
```

Or

```
Please let me know if there are any changes or we are good to go.
Thanks!
```

That way (we hope) you will know your segment hasn't been cancelled without your knowledge, or key details changed, such as the time or length of the segment. Make sure the producer has your cell number so he or she can reach you at the last minute, if necessary. If you and your client are traveling separately to the TV station for the segment, give the producer your client's cell number, too, and get any parking information (Do they need a pass? Is there a guard at the gate?). Let the client know where to meet you at the station (parking lot, lobby, or green room, for example) and give them clear directions to the station, the parking info, and the producer's name and contact number. You don't want to leave either the client or the producer hanging if your phone dies or your car breaks down that morning.

How To Prepare for and Make the Most of a TV News Appearance

One client who was not local insisted on driving himself everywhere in his rental car. More than once he would get lost, and always blamed me. After being dressed down by him one too many times, I learned he needed maps and directions printed out ahead of time. These days, GPS saves us all the trouble.

4.
Be On Time

Arrive on time, or a bit early. The news producer will have given you two times when confirming your segment: arrival time and on-air time. The first is when they would like you to physically be present at the station; the second is when your segment is expected to start.

Be there by your arrival time, even if you don't think you need a lot of set-up and it's likely you're going to stand around waiting. The producers need to know you're there and ready so they have one less thing to worry about during the newscast. There's also a chance their schedule might change and they need you to go on earlier than planned. Be flexible; if they're in a jam and your client is there and ready to jump in, they'll appreciate it.

Time spent waiting for your segment is also time you can spend getting to know some of the TV station staff or other guests waiting their turns in the green room.

I once spent 45 minutes with a client waiting in a TV station green room to do a live segment, and during that time he was able to secure a $10,000 donation for his cause from an executive who was also waiting in the green room to do a segment of her own.

5.
Or, Arrive Early

If your segment requires a lot of set-up, arrive early. Try to anticipate the unexpected that could delay your being ready when it's time to do the live segment. Think through the process. Does the client have to get into a costume, or finish doing his or her hair and makeup? Are you presenting a cooking segment that requires decorating the table, food prep, pans heated up, and plating? Do you need to provide and cue up a CD of music, or set up musical instruments and do a sound check for a live performance? Are you and your client going to assemble an elaborate table display?

If any of these is the case, or there are other possibilities that mean extra time would be required, arrive well before your scheduled arrival time, and get set up as soon as the TV station staff will let you. As we covered in section 4, it's good to be ready and available early in case of scheduling changes. But it also gives you some wiggle room, in case you've forgotten anything or something else goes wrong. On several occasions I've had chef clients realize as they're setting up that they forgot to pack a key ingredient or tool, and because we were there early, we had the time to either race back to the restaurant to fetch it, or call and have a coworker bring it to the station in time.

Also as mentioned in section IV, being set up and ready early gives you time to network. Delicious cooking smells or musical warm-ups are a great advertisement for your client to everyone within smelling or hearing range.

One client forgot to bring to an interview a model airplane his students had been working on that was crucial to the segment. We arrived about half an hour early. The model was in his garage at his home. He called his daughters and they jumped in the car with the model. The segment, which was outdoors, began. As the client was answering the first question, I saw his daughter's car pulling up in the parking lot. I ran over and grabbed the model, and by the third question, I was able to hand it to him discreetly from just out of camera range.

6.
Dress For Success

You and your client should be aware of some details about appearing on television. To begin with, remember that you really will look heavier on camera—it's not a myth. If you or your client is concerned about that, your best bet is to wear solidly dark, fitted clothes. It should go without saying that your client should wear clean, pressed, professional attire that is appropriate to the segment you're doing, but if you sense one of the people who will be on camera might need a gentle reminder, provide it (politely). For example, it's perfectly appropriate for the designer of a new line of skatewear to wear skateboarding shorts and a t-shirt on TV—as long as the shorts and t-shirt are clean and intact. The same goes for chef jackets—they should be spotless and crisp.

Unless you're a chef, don't wear white. It registers too bright to the TV cameras and throws off their lighting balance. Don't wear any clothing with a small check or plaid pattern; it will give a moiré or ripple effect on camera.

Avoid stripes, zig-zags, and wild patterns or bright florals. None of these registers well on TV and they are distracting to look at. Bright colors are fine, but stick to solids, and not too many colors at the same time.

Woman-identifying persons who will be speaking during the segment should try to avoid wearing a clingy dress or other clothing that will not provide anywhere to hook a wireless microphone pack. A mic pack is about the size of a small cell phone, and they will ask you to clip it onto your clothes somewhere out of sight, usually the back of your pants or skirt. You'll then be asked to run a wire up through your clothing and pop the small mic out of your neckline, clipping it onto your neckline or collar. For that reason, you should avoid wearing a clunky necklace or swishy scarf that might interfere with it. That's also why you shouldn't wear a turtleneck, unless you're wearing a jacket over it.

The TV station will not provide a hair and makeup artist for you, or even take into account the time you might need to do your hair and apply makeup, so make sure you do that before you arrive. Clients who usually wear makeup should go a little heavier on it that morning. If you or your client don't normally wear makeup, consider doing so for a TV appearance. It makes you look less washed-out on screen, especially next to a news anchor or reporter, who will all be heavily made up. Practice before the day of the segment, so you get the look you want and are comfortable with it.

Those who don't want to wear any makeup can still benefit from a light dusting of powder so they look less shiny on camera, especially if they have a tendency to perspire. The studio may feel cold, but it's hot under the lights, or in the sun for an outdoor segment, and being nervous doesn't help. Most media reps carry some makeup basics with them to help out a client in a pinch.

I believe in being over-prepared. When going with a client to a TV segment, in addition to makeup, I always bring safety pins, Band-Aids, eye drops, a comb and hairspray. I also bring supporting materials for the segment, the client's business cards as well as mine, and a cell phone battery pack and charge cord.

One time in the green room a client spilled coffee on her blouse and I had to quickly switch tops with her. Ever since then, I also carry a fairly neutral-colored scarf, just in case something needs to be covered up.

7.
Don't Wander Off

The TV station staff will show you to the green room and get you settled. They will come back for you when it's time for you and your client to move to the studio and get set up. Unless you know your way around that particular TV news station very well, it's best that you don't wander the halls. It's very easy to get lost in the warren of offices, studios, storerooms, and editing bays.

Stay put until they come get you, and make sure one of the news staff shows you exactly where to go. If you need the restroom, ask where it is as soon as you arrive, and follow directions. You don't want to disrupt people at work or wander into a sensitive area by mistake. Go through the wrong door and you may well find yourself walking onto the set in the middle of the live news broadcast—or locked out in the parking lot.

8.
Observe Studio Etiquette

Especially if you haven't been in one before, a television station can be an intimidating environment. There are some simple things you can do to make the whole experience less nerve-racking for you and your client, and easier on the TV station staff.

First of all, turn off your cell phones' ringers as soon as you arrive, and double-check that they're really silenced. If possible, leave your phones in the green room when you're called into the studio. If you have to take them with you, turn them off completely for the whole time you're in the studio, whether you're on camera or not.

Try not to talk while you're in the studio. If you have to, whisper. It can be hard to tell when the cameras are on. The station's staff may or may not bother to let you know when they're live and rolling. You don't want to inadvertently be heard talking during the newscast, or distract the anchors and reporters. This will especially reflect poorly on you, the PR pro, who should know better.

If your client is setting up a display, or warming up to sing or perform, check with the production staff and do it carefully, only when you're told it's clear. Stand where you are told, out of the way, and try not to move around too much. Camera operators may need to move suddenly. Some TV studio cameras are fully automated now, and will move across the floor, unattended, without warning. Again, you don't want to be a distraction by being in the wrong place, or end up on camera by accident.

9.
Relax, Be Yourself

When it's your and/or your client's turn to be on camera, be ready and alert as soon as you're in position. Act naturally; be yourself. Speak in your normal voice and address the anchor or reporter as if you were having a regular conversation. This is important, and a common rookie mistake: Don't look into or address the camera unless specifically directed to. If not seated, stay in one spot. If you aren't doing anything with your hands for the segment, keep them still. Try not to fiddle with anything or gesticulate much.

Listen to the questions carefully and try to pick up on your interviewer's cues to have a friendly, lively chat. On the other hand, don't assume your interviewer has memorized all the information you sent them ahead of time, or will have time to cover it all. Some reporters and anchors do lots of research and prepare thoroughly ahead of time; others may have not even glanced at your info until 30 seconds before the interview begins.

Even the most conscientious ones have busy days or bad days. They are reporting on dozens of stories each day, and although your segment is the only important one to you, it's just one of many to them. Be flexible, and be prepared to fill in blanks for them. If the interview is coming to a close and you realize a key point you wanted to make is going to be missed, try to work it in without being too obvious. For example:

```
Anchor: So, again, the festival is this weekend at the Del Mar
Fairgrounds..?
Client:  That's right, from 10 a.m. to 6 p.m.—and parking is free!
```

If the interview goes in a direction you didn't expect and aren't happy with, try to steer it back to where you want it. Seasoned interview subjects learn to hit all their bullet points and communicate the information they want to, regardless of the questions they are asked, sometimes with a brief comment that provides a segue, sometimes just by flat-out changing the subject. This takes finesse and is best developed with time. But in most cases it won't be necessary. Most TV reporters or anchors are happy to let you tell your story and help you get the word out, and are not out to trick or trap you. (Unless your client is in damage control mode, but that's a different conversation.)

Finally, if the interviewer makes an error during your segment, and it's an important one (like the wrong date or location for an event, or the wrong website for more info), respond by quickly giving the correct information and move on. Don't make a big deal about it.

While your client is being interviewed and you're off-camera, try to watch a monitor so you see what the audience at home is seeing. That way, if you notice incorrect information posted on the screen during the interview or something else amiss, you can politely notify the producers immediately so they can correct it as soon as possible, preferably while the interview is still on the air, and definitely before it goes up on the web.

10.
Share the Goodies

Everybody likes free food. If your segment includes food, bring plastic serveware and plenty of extra supplies. If it was fully cooked and up to your client's standards, leave behind the food that was prepared during the segment for the staff and crew to enjoy. (You're just going to have to throw it away, anyway.) If they decline, leave it anyway. Someone will definitely enjoy it in the end.

If you have samples of a product you can give away, bring lots of that. If you're promoting an event, bring as many free tickets as you can to hand out or leave in the staff room.

Make sure your client brings business cards or flyers to leave in the green room and break room along with the freebies. TV staff members talk and spread the word online. Lots of word of mouth can be generated by giving them the info and something to remember you by.

11.
Work the Room

This may seem obvious, but be polite and friendly to *everyone* at the station. TV news station staffers move around a lot. This week's intern could be next month's assistant segment producer. The sound technician at one station could be hired next week at a different station, one you haven't been able to crack yet. Assistant producers get promoted. They work with a lot of guests and publicists, but they remember the nice ones—and the ones that weren't so nice, too.

12.
Make Your Exit

When your segment is over, ask the producer if they need you to stick around for anything. Especially with a food demo or performance-oriented segment, if they liked it, they might ask you to stay and help close out the show, which just gives your client more airtime.

When you're completely done, thank everyone and clear out as quickly as you can. Remember to be as quiet as you can if the newscast is continuing. Don't hang around; you'll just be in the way. They are already moving on to the next segment and forgetting about you.

Follow up right away, the same day if possible, with a thank-you to the producer who booked you. Be specific—mention something that was particularly fun about the segment that made it go well, or how helpful it will be to your group or organization to have appeared on the news.

Within a few hours, you can start checking if the news station has posted the news segment on their website. As soon as the segment is up, post the link on your website and social media sites, and ask your client to do the same. This gives you an opportunity to communicate with the producer again, to let them know you're helping spread the word. They will appreciate the additional promotion you're providing for their newscast.

13.
Swallow Your Disappointment

If the worst happens and your segment is canceled, whether ahead of time or at the last minute, even if you're already onsite and all set up, don't react badly. It's the nature of live TV news that things happen quickly, and nothing is set in stone. Breaking news or changes in another segment can mean your segment is no longer able to fit in the newscast.

Be gracious. If the segment is not time-sensitive and your client is open to it, make it clear to the producer that you're happy to reschedule at their earliest convenience. They will probably want to make it up to you, since they were interested enough to book you in the first place. In any case, they'll remember that you handled it well and didn't give them grief for something that was most likely out of their control.

14.
Give Thanks and Feedback

Sometimes, despite all your careful planning and preparation, the segment may not turn out the way you hoped. Take a little time to think about it, and consider whether it's worth bringing it up to the producer after the fact. Depending on how much damage was done, sometimes it's better to let it go. Some producers will appreciate a polite comment about how things could have been handled better. The more experienced you are and the more you get to know them, the better you will be able to judge whether it's the right way to go.

If you decide to make the call, do it within a day or two, so it's fresh in everyone's minds. Keep it short, cordial, and specific, without belaboring the point. Make sure they know you are communicating your client's disappointment in how the segment turned out. Keep your tone light and friendly. Again, your client may be upset enough to not care if they ever again work with this TV station, but the PR rep can't afford to burn any bridges.

This is one of the few times when calling on the phone is probably better than writing it out in an email, which can seem too formal. If you get their voicemail, make your points in a message, without asking them to return the call. Producers are busy, and no one wants to call someone back just to hear them complain.

Most of the time, though, the segment will be a success. The next time you pitch the same producer, remind him or her how great it was to work with them last time. You'll find yourself invited back sooner than later.

About the Author

Stephanie Saad Thompson has more than 30 years of experience as a public relations consultant and practitioner. She has worked with a wide variety of clients, from multinational corporations to small nonprofits, and from performing arts, festivals, and nationally touring entertainment to medical clinics, retail, and the service and hospitality industry.

Stephanie has consulted with corporations and nonprofit organizations in the areas of media strategies, social media planning and implementation, special event planning, crisis communications, and executive media training. After eight years heading the media relations department at a major San Diego performing arts organization, where she led a number of successful and award-winning communications initiatives, Stephanie formed and led her own public relations agency for 20 years. She was previously a newspaper writer and editor, and is also a copy editor. She is now Communications and Public Relations Director for La Jolla Music Society.

Thank you to ML Hart and Reema Makani Boccia, first readers.

www.ingramcontent.com/pod-product-compliance
Lightning Source LLC
Chambersburg PA
CBHW060023300526
45794CB00003B/1266